GUARDIANS OF THE NET:
A COMPLETE GUIDE TO CYBERSECURITY

BY

SABAT BEATTO

TABLE OF CONTENTS

CHAPTER 1:
INTRODUCTION TO CYBERSECURITY

Overview of Cybersecurity

In the dawn of the digital era, cybersecurity has emerged as a cornerstone of modern society, a bastion safeguarding the integrity, confidentiality, and availability of information that fuels our daily lives. Cybersecurity, at its core, is the practice of protecting systems, networks, and programs from digital attacks. These cyberattacks typically aim to access, change, or destroy sensitive information, extort money from users, or interrupt normal business processes.

The realm of cybersecurity is vast and intricate, encompassing a range of practices, solutions, and technologies designed to fend off attacks that come in many forms. These include malware, ransomware, phishing, and more sophisticated forms of cybercrime. The landscape of cyber threats is continuously evolving, with attackers becoming more innovative in their methods.

Cybersecurity isn't just a technical challenge; it's also a critical strategic issue. It involves understanding the risk landscape, adhering to regulatory and legal requirements, and aligning security measures with business objectives. This broad spectrum necessitates a multidisciplinary approach, integrating technical expertise with an understanding of governance, law, psychology, and more.

Importance in the Modern World

In today's interconnected world, the importance of cybersecurity cannot be overstated. Our reliance on technology in personal, professional, and governmental realms makes us vulnerable to a myriad of cyber threats. From banking to healthcare, education to national security, every sector is reliant on the safety and reliability of digital systems.

The consequences of cyberattacks are profound. They can lead to the theft of sensitive personal and financial information, disrupt critical infrastructure, and even compromise national security. The economic impact is equally significant, with businesses incurring substantial losses due to downtime, data breaches, and the cost of recovery.

Moreover, in an age where data is a valuable commodity, the protection of personal privacy has become a paramount concern. Cybersecurity is essential in safeguarding personal data from unauthorized access and ensuring compliance with privacy laws.

The digital landscape is not static; it evolves rapidly, as do the threats that inhabit it. The future of cybersecurity is a journey towards more sophisticated defensive technologies like artificial intelligence and machine learning, which promise to revolutionize the way we protect our digital assets. This ongoing evolution makes cybersecurity not just a technical necessity but a continuous learning process for professionals in the field.

As we delve deeper into the digital age, the importance of cybersecurity is only set to grow. It stands as the guardian of our digital frontier, a critical component that underpins the safety and functionality of our increasingly connected world.

CHAPTER 2:
HISTORICAL EVOLUTION OF CYBERSECURITY

Early Days of Internet Security

The journey of cybersecurity begins with the genesis of the internet. In the late 1960s and early 1970s, when the internet was in its embryonic stage as ARPANET, security was not a primary concern. The network was limited to a small group of trusted users. However, as the network expanded, the need for security measures became apparent. The first recorded cybersecurity incident was the Creeper virus in 1971, a harmless experimental self-replicating program, marking the advent of what would become network security.

The 1980s saw the rise of the personal computer and with it, the birth of malicious software – malware. The era was marked by the emergence of computer viruses and worms. Notable among them was the Brain virus (1986), often considered the first computer virus for MS-DOS, which signified a shift towards awareness about the vulnerabilities in software and the need for protective measures.

The 1990s brought the internet to the general public, and with this democratization came a proliferation of cyber threats. The decade saw a significant evolution in the complexity and impact of cyberattacks.

The Morris Worm, released in 1988, was one of the first worms distributed via the internet, bringing to light the potential scale of cyber threats. This incident underscored the need for cybersecurity awareness and the development of more robust security protocols.

Major Historical Cyber Attacks

The history of cybersecurity is dotted with landmark cyberattacks that have reshaped our understanding of digital vulnerabilities.

1. **ILOVEYOU Worm (2000):** This infamous virus, masquerading as a love letter attached in an email, wreaked havoc globally, infecting millions of computers and causing billions in damages. It highlighted the vulnerability of software systems and the ease with which a virus can spread through social engineering.

2. **Sony Pictures Hack (2014):** A watershed event in corporate cybersecurity, this attack not only led to a massive data breach but also brought to light the concept of state-sponsored cyberattacks. The incident raised concerns about the need for stronger corporate cybersecurity measures.

3. **WannaCry Ransomware Attack (2017):** Affecting over 200,000 computers across 150 countries, this ransomware encrypted data and demanded ransom payments in Bitcoin. It exploited vulnerabilities in older Windows systems, underscoring the importance of regular software updates and patches.

These attacks, among others, have shaped the cybersecurity landscape, driving the development of more advanced security measures and policies. They have also highlighted the importance of a proactive approach to cybersecurity, emphasizing the need for continuous monitoring, updating, and refining of security strategies.

Conclusion

The historical evolution of cybersecurity is a narrative of an arms race between cyber defenders and attackers. From the early days of internet security, where threats were rare and relatively benign, to the present day, where cyberattacks can have global repercussions, the field of cybersecurity has continually evolved. This history is not just a record of past challenges but a guide to understanding the ever-changing landscape of digital threats. It teaches us the importance of vigilance, adaptation, and the relentless pursuit of stronger, more effective cybersecurity measures.

CHAPTER 3:
FUNDAMENTALS OF CYBERSECURITY

Introduction

At the heart of protecting our digital world lies the fundamentals of cybersecurity. This chapter delves into the basic concepts that form the bedrock of cybersecurity practices, focusing on essential principles like encryption, network security, and more. Understanding these concepts is crucial for anyone venturing into the realm of cybersecurity, whether as a practitioner, a student, or a concerned individual in the digital age.

Encryption: The Art of Secret Communication

Encryption is a cornerstone of cybersecurity. It's the process of converting information or data into a code to prevent unauthorized access. This cryptographic technique secures digital data, communications, and information stored on devices or transmitted across networks.

Two main types of encryption are widely used: Symmetric encryption, where the same key is used for both encryption and decryption, and Asymmetric encryption, which uses a pair of public and private keys. This foundational concept underpins various cybersecurity applications, from securing emails to protecting data stored on the cloud.

Network Security: Guarding the Digital Perimeter

Network security is a broad term that covers a multitude of technologies, devices, and processes. It's the practice of securing a computer network from intruders, whether they are opportunistic attackers or targeted threats. Network security involves implementing both hardware and software mechanisms.

Key elements of network security include:

- **Firewalls:** A barrier between a trusted and an untrusted network.

- **Intrusion Prevention Systems (IPS):** Monitors network traffic to detect and prevent attacks.

- **Virtual Private Networks (VPNs):** Creates a secure connection over a public network.

- **Anti-Virus and Anti-Malware Software:** Protects against software threats.

Understanding Malware and Its Defenses

Malware, or malicious software, is any program or file that harms a computer user. Types of malware include viruses, worms, Trojan horses, and ransomware. Understanding how these threats operate is critical for effective defense strategies.

Cybersecurity measures against malware include:

- Regular software updates to patch vulnerabilities.
- Antivirus software to detect and remove threats.
- User education to avoid phishing attacks and suspicious downloads.

The Importance of Secure Passwords and Authentication

A strong password is a user's first line of defense against unauthorized access. Password security involves creating complex, unique passwords and changing them regularly. Additionally, Multi-Factor Authentication (MFA) adds an extra layer of security by requiring two or more verification methods.

Data Security: Protecting the Crown Jewels

Data security involves protecting data from unauthorized access and corruption throughout its lifecycle. Key practices include:

- Data encryption.
- Secure storage solutions.
- Access controls.
- Regular backups.

Emerging Trends: AI and Machine Learning in Cybersecurity

The field of cybersecurity is constantly evolving, with Artificial Intelligence (AI) and Machine Learning (ML) playing increasingly significant roles. These technologies are being used for automated threat detection, pattern recognition, and predicting potential vulnerabilities.

Conclusion

Understanding the fundamentals of cybersecurity is akin to learning the alphabet before writing a novel. These basic concepts form the underpinning of all cybersecurity practices and strategies. As the digital landscape evolves, so do the threats that challenge its integrity. A solid grasp of cybersecurity fundamentals is essential for anyone looking to navigate this ever-changing terrain, ensuring the protection of digital assets in an increasingly interconnected world.

CHAPTER 4:
TYPES OF CYBER THREATS

Introduction

In the digital age, understanding the types of cyber threats is crucial for developing effective defense strategies. This chapter provides a comprehensive overview of various cyber threats, such as viruses, malware, phishing, and more, which are critical for anyone in the field of cybersecurity to understand.

Viruses and Worms: The Classics of Cyber Threats

A computer virus is a type of malicious code or program written to alter the way a computer operates and is designed to spread from one computer to another. It can replicate itself and spread by attaching to other programs. Worms are similar but can spread themselves without needing to attach to a host program.

These threats can:

- Corrupt or modify files.

- Steal sensitive information.

- Cause system crashes or slowdowns.

Malware: A Broad and Evolving Threat

Malware, short for malicious software, encompasses various forms of harmful software designed to attack, damage, or disable computers and computer systems. It includes viruses, worms, Trojan horses, ransomware, spyware, adware, and scareware.

Each type has its unique behavior:

- **Trojan horses** disguise themselves as legitimate software.

- **Ransomware** locks or encrypts data, demanding a ransom for its release.

- **Spyware** surreptitiously gathers user information.

Phishing: The Art of Deception

Phishing is a cyber threat that involves tricking individuals into divulging sensitive information, such as login credentials or credit card numbers, by masquerading as a trustworthy entity in digital communication. It often involves emails or messages that mimic legitimate organizations.

Phishing tactics can include:

- Fake websites that resemble legitimate ones.

- Urgent or threatening language to provoke quick action.

- Requests for personal or financial information.

DDoS Attacks: Disruption on a Massive Scale

Distributed Denial of Service (DDoS) attacks aim to disrupt normal web traffic and take a targeted website offline by overwhelming the site with a flood of internet traffic. These attacks can cripple websites, causing significant downtime and loss of business.

Man-in-the-Middle (MitM) Attacks: Intercepting Communications

MitM attacks occur when attackers insert themselves into a two-party transaction or communication. Once inserted, attackers can filter and steal data. Common types include session hijacking and Wi-Fi eavesdropping.

Zero-Day Exploits: The Unknown Threat

Zero-day exploits target software vulnerabilities that are unknown to those interested in mitigating the vulnerability, including the vendor of the target software. These attacks are particularly dangerous because they occur before the vulnerability is known, giving no time for patching or mitigation.

Insider Threats: Danger from Within

Insider threats come from individuals within an organization, such as employees or contractors, who misuse their access to harm the organization. This can involve stealing information, sabotaging systems, or aiding external attackers.

Emerging Threats: AI and IoT

As technology evolves, new threats emerge. Artificial Intelligence (AI) is being used to create more sophisticated cyber-attacks, while the proliferation of Internet of Things (IoT) devices has opened new avenues for exploitation due to often inadequate security measures.

Conclusion

Understanding the types of cyber threats is paramount in the fight against cybercrime. This chapter not only outlines the various forms of threats but also emphasizes the need for ongoing vigilance and adaptation in cybersecurity strategies. As the landscape of digital threats continues to evolve, so must our approaches to defending against them. Knowledge of these threats is a critical step in building a secure digital world.

CHAPTER 5:
CYBERSECURITY TECHNOLOGIES

Introduction

The field of cybersecurity is bolstered by an array of technologies designed to protect digital systems and networks from unauthorized access, attacks, and damages. This chapter explores key cybersecurity technologies such as firewalls, anti-virus software, and intrusion detection systems, explaining their roles, functionalities, and importance in the modern cybersecurity landscape.

Firewalls: The First Line of Defense

Firewalls are one of the most fundamental cybersecurity technologies. They act as a barrier between trusted internal networks and untrusted external networks, such as the Internet. A firewall uses a set of defined rules to allow or block traffic into and out of the network.

Types of firewalls include:

- **Packet-filtering firewalls,** the most basic type, which inspect packets of data as they are transmitted across the network.

- **Stateful inspection firewalls,** which monitor the state of active connections and make decisions based on the context of traffic.

- **Next-generation firewalls (NGFWs),** which offer more advanced features like application-level inspection, intrusion prevention, and cloud-delivered threat intelligence.

Anti-Virus and Anti-Malware Software: Guarding Against Software Threats

Anti-virus software is essential for detecting, preventing, and removing malware. These programs scan the computer's memory and disk drives regularly for known types of malware and patterns indicative of new malware.

Key features of anti-virus software include:

- **Real-time scanning** to detect malware activities as they occur.

- **Heuristic analysis** to identify previously unknown viruses or variants.

- **Automatic updates** to ensure protection against the latest threats.

Intrusion Detection and Prevention Systems (IDPS): Monitoring and Responding to Threats

IDPS are critical for identifying potential threats and responding to them swiftly. Intrusion Detection Systems (IDS) monitor network or system activities for malicious activities or policy violations, while Intrusion Prevention Systems (IPS) actively prevent or block these threats.

IDPS functionalities include:

- **Signature-based detection,** which uses known patterns of malicious activity.

- **Anomaly-based detection,** which compares against an established baseline to identify abnormal activities.

- **Policy-based detection,** which uses predefined security policies to identify deviations.

Encryption Technologies: Ensuring Data Privacy

Encryption technologies play a vital role in protecting data privacy. They transform readable data into an unreadable format, which can only be reverted by authorized parties.

Encryption is used in:

- **Data encryption** to protect data at rest, in transit, or in use.

- **End-to-end encryption** in messaging and communication apps.

- **Public Key Infrastructure (PKI)** for secure electronic transfer of information.

Secure Socket Layer (SSL) and Transport Layer Security (TLS): Safe Internet Communication

SSL and TLS protocols provide secure communications over a computer network. Websites use SSL/TLS to secure all communications between their servers and web browsers, essential for protecting sensitive data during online transactions.

Cloud Security Technologies

With the increasing adoption of cloud computing, cloud security technologies have become essential. They include data encryption, identity and access management, and security information and event management (SIEM) systems tailored for the cloud environment.

Conclusion

Cybersecurity technologies form the backbone of efforts to protect digital assets and infrastructures. From firewalls to encryption, each technology plays a unique role in safeguarding information systems. As cyber threats evolve, so do these technologies, requiring continuous adaptation and improvement. Understanding these technologies is vital for anyone involved in the field of cybersecurity, providing the tools and knowledge necessary to defend against the ever-changing landscape of cyber threats.

CHAPTER 6:
ETHICAL HACKING AND DEFENSE STRATEGIES

Introduction

In the complex world of cybersecurity, defending against threats requires an understanding of how attackers operate. This is where ethical hacking and defense strategies play a pivotal role. Ethical hacking involves legally breaking into computers and devices to test an organization's defenses. This chapter explores the realm of ethical hacking, focusing on penetration testing and the fundamentals of ethical hacking as proactive defense strategies.

The Concept of Ethical Hacking

Ethical hacking, also known as white-hat hacking, is the practice of bypassing system security to identify potential data breaches and threats in a network. The key difference between ethical and malicious hacking lies in permission; ethical hackers have authorization to probe and exploit security networks and improve defense mechanisms.

Penetration Testing: Simulating Cyber Attacks

Penetration testing, or pen testing, is a core component of ethical hacking. It involves simulating cyberattacks to identify vulnerabilities in a system, network, or web application. Pen tests can be classified into different types, including:

- **Black Box Testing:** The tester has no prior knowledge of the network infrastructure.

- **White Box Testing:** The tester has complete knowledge of the infrastructure.

- **Grey Box Testing:** A combination of both black and white box testing, where some knowledge is provided.

Phases of Penetration Testing

A typical pen test includes several stages:

1. **Planning and Reconnaissance:** Defining the scope and gathering intelligence.

2. **Scanning:** Understanding how the target application will respond to various intrusion attempts.

3. **Gaining Access:** Using web application attacks, such as cross-site scripting, SQL injection, and backdoors, to uncover vulnerabilities.

4. **Maintaining Access:** Seeing if the vulnerability can be used to achieve a persistent presence in the exploited system, mimicking advanced persistent threats.

5. **Analysis:** Documenting the vulnerabilities discovered and providing recommendations for mitigation.

Tools and Techniques in Ethical Hacking

Ethical hackers employ a variety of tools and techniques to probe and test systems and networks. These include:

- **Network Scanners:** To identify live hosts, open ports, and other details of the network.

- **Vulnerability Scanners:** To automatically scan for vulnerabilities.

- **Packet Sniffers:** To capture and analyze network traffic.

- **Exploitation Tools:** To exploit identified vulnerabilities.

Ethical Hacking Basics: Skills and Knowledge

Fundamental skills for ethical hackers include a deep understanding of networking, databases, hardware, and software systems. Knowledge of programming and scripting languages is also advantageous.

Legal and Ethical Considerations

Ethical hacking is governed by legal and ethical guidelines. Hackers must have explicit permission to probe systems and should respect the scope of their authorization, ensuring confidentiality and integrity of the data.

Conclusion

Ethical hacking and defense strategies are essential in the cybersecurity ecosystem. They provide insights into potential vulnerabilities and allow organizations to fortify their defenses proactively. As technology evolves, so does the scope of ethical hacking, requiring continuous learning and adaptation to stay ahead of potential threats. This chapter not only educates on the methodologies and tools of ethical hacking but also emphasizes its critical role in strengthening cybersecurity defenses.

CHAPTER 7:
CYBERSECURITY IN DIFFERENT SECTORS

Introduction

Cybersecurity is not a one-size-fits-all domain. Different sectors face unique challenges and threats, requiring tailored security strategies. This chapter explores the cybersecurity landscape across various critical sectors, including government, healthcare, finance, and more, highlighting their specific needs and the approaches to safeguarding their digital assets.

Government Sector: Safeguarding National Security

The government sector is a prime target for cyberattacks due to the sensitive nature of the information it holds. Cybersecurity in this sector is crucial for protecting classified data, maintaining national security, and ensuring the integrity of public services.

Key challenges include:

- Protecting against espionage and state-sponsored attacks.

- Securing critical infrastructure like power grids and transportation.

- Implementing comprehensive policies for data protection and information sharing.

Healthcare Sector: Protecting Patient Data

The healthcare sector deals with highly sensitive patient data, making it a lucrative target for cybercriminals. The increasing adoption of electronic health records (EHRs) and medical IoT devices has further amplified the risks.

Cybersecurity challenges in healthcare involve:

- Ensuring the confidentiality and integrity of patient records.

- Protecting against ransomware attacks that can cripple hospital systems.

- Complying with health data protection regulations like HIPAA.

Financial Sector: Guarding Financial Stability

The financial sector, encompassing banks, investment firms, and insurance companies, is inherently attractive to cybercriminals due to the monetary gains involved. The sector is also a backbone of economic stability, making its protection critical.

Cybersecurity in finance focuses on:

- Preventing fraud and theft of financial data.

- Securing online transactions and banking platforms.

- Complying with financial industry regulations and standards.

Retail and E-Commerce: Safeguarding Consumer Trust

The retail and e-commerce sector faces cybersecurity challenges primarily related to consumer data protection and online transaction security. With the surge in online shopping, ensuring a secure shopping environment is crucial.

Key areas of focus include:

- Protecting customer data and privacy.

- Preventing breaches in online payment systems.

- Maintaining website security to thwart attacks like DDoS.

Manufacturing and Industrial Sector: Securing Operational Technology

Cybersecurity in the manufacturing and industrial sectors is increasingly important due to the rise of Industry 4.0 and the integration of operational technology (OT) with information technology (IT). The sector is facing new challenges with the advent of smart manufacturing and IoT.

Concerns in this sector involve:

- Protecting industrial control systems (ICS) and SCADA systems.

- Securing interconnected manufacturing processes.

- Preventing disruption of physical operations through cyber means.

Education Sector: Defending Intellectual Property

Educational institutions are repositories of valuable research and personal data, making them targets for cyberattacks. Balancing open access to information with security is a unique challenge in this sector.

Cybersecurity in education must address:

- Protecting student and staff data.

- Securing research data and intellectual property.

- Ensuring secure online learning platforms.

Conclusion

Cybersecurity needs and strategies vary significantly across different sectors. Each sector faces unique challenges and threats, requiring tailored cybersecurity measures. This chapter not only highlights the distinct cybersecurity landscapes of various sectors but also emphasizes the need for sector-specific strategies to effectively mitigate risks and protect against cyber threats. Understanding these nuances is crucial for cybersecurity professionals who must adapt their skills and knowledge to the specific requirements of the sector they are serving.

CHAPTER 8:
DATA PRIVACY AND PROTECTION LAWS

Introduction

In the digital age, data privacy and protection have become paramount. With increasing cyber threats and data breaches, various countries and regions have enacted laws to safeguard personal data. This chapter delves into key regulations like the General Data Protection Regulation (GDPR), California Consumer Privacy Act (CCPA), and other significant global data protection laws, examining their impact on businesses and individuals.

General Data Protection Regulation (GDPR): A European Benchmark

The GDPR, implemented in May 2018, is a groundbreaking data protection regulation in the European Union (EU). It has set a high standard for data privacy worldwide, impacting not only European businesses but also global companies that handle EU citizens' data.

Key aspects of GDPR include:

- **Consent:** Individuals must explicitly consent to the collection and use of their personal data.

- **Right to Access:** Individuals have the right to know what personal data is stored about them and how it is processed.

- **Data Portability:** Individuals can transfer their personal data from one service provider to another.

- **Right to Be Forgotten:** Individuals can request the deletion of their personal data.

Non-compliance with GDPR can result in hefty fines, making it a significant consideration for businesses globally.

California Consumer Privacy Act (CCPA): America's Forefront in Data Privacy

The CCPA, effective from January 2020, is the most comprehensive data privacy law in the United States. It applies to any business that collects the personal information of California residents and meets certain criteria.

CCPA's key provisions include:

- **Disclosure:** Businesses must disclose the categories of personal information they collect and the purposes for which they use it.

- **Opt-Out Right:** Consumers can opt out of the sale of their personal information.

- **Right to Deletion:** Consumers can request the deletion of their personal information.

Other Global Data Protection Regulations

- **The Personal Information Protection and Electronic Documents Act (PIPEDA) in Canada:** Sets out how businesses must handle personal information in the course of commercial activities.

- **The Data Protection Act in the UK:** Post-Brexit, the UK has its own version of data protection legislation, mirroring many of GDPR's principles.

- **Brazil's General Data Protection Law (LGPD):** Similar to GDPR, it regulates the processing of personal data of individuals in Brazil.

Impact on Businesses and Compliance Challenges

These laws have a profound impact on how businesses collect, store, process, and share personal data. Compliance involves:

- Implementing robust data protection measures.

- Ensuring transparency in data processing activities.

- Training staff on data protection best practices.

Emerging Trends and Future Directions

As digital data continues to explode, more countries are likely to introduce stringent data protection laws. Additionally, existing laws may evolve to address new challenges posed by emerging technologies like AI and IoT.

Conclusion

Data privacy and protection laws play a crucial role in shaping the way organizations handle personal data. Understanding these laws is essential for compliance and for protecting the rights of individuals in the digital world. As the landscape of data privacy continues to evolve, staying informed and agile in adapting to new regulations will be vital for businesses and cybersecurity professionals alike. This chapter provides a comprehensive overview of the key laws and their implications, serving as a guide in navigating the complex world of data privacy and protection.

CHAPTER 9:
THE ROLE OF ARTIFICIAL INTELLIGENCE IN CYBERSECURITY

Introduction

In the rapidly evolving domain of cybersecurity, Artificial Intelligence (AI) has emerged as a transformative force. AI's ability to process vast amounts of data at unprecedented speeds is revolutionizing how cybersecurity threats are detected and responded to. This chapter delves into the integration of AI in cybersecurity, focusing on its role in threat detection and response.

AI in Cyber Threat Detection

One of the most significant applications of AI in cybersecurity is in the detection of threats and anomalies. AI systems equipped with machine learning algorithms can analyze patterns and behaviors within massive datasets, identifying potential threats more efficiently than traditional methods.

Key aspects of AI in threat detection include:

- **Anomaly Detection:** AI algorithms can identify deviations from normal network behavior, which may indicate a cyber attack.

- **Predictive Analysis:** AI can predict future threats by analyzing current and historical security data.

- **Pattern Recognition:** AI excels in recognizing complex patterns in data, which is crucial in detecting sophisticated cyber threats.

AI-Driven Intrusion Detection Systems

Advanced intrusion detection systems (IDS) powered by AI are capable of identifying even the most subtle and novel attacks. These systems learn from existing data and continuously evolve, adapting to new and emerging threats.

Enhancing Malware Detection with AI

AI has significantly improved the efficacy of malware detection. Traditional antivirus solutions rely on signature-based detection, but AI allows for the identification of malware based on behavior, making it more effective against zero-day attacks.

AI in Cybersecurity Response

Once a threat is detected, an immediate and effective response is crucial. AI technologies streamline response procedures in several ways:

- **Automated Incident Response:** AI can automate certain responses to common threats, reducing the time and resources required to address them.

- **Decision Support:** AI can provide cybersecurity professionals with actionable insights and recommendations for threat mitigation.

- **Threat Hunting:** AI can proactively search for potential threats within a network before they manifest into attacks.

Challenges and Ethical Considerations

While AI offers immense potential in cybersecurity, it also presents challenges:

- **False Positives and Negatives:** Reliance on AI can lead to misidentification of threats, either by overreacting to benign activities or missing malicious ones.

- **AI Security:** AI systems themselves can become targets for cybercriminals.

- **Ethical Concerns:** The use of AI in cybersecurity raises ethical questions, particularly around privacy and data use.

Future of AI in Cybersecurity

The future of AI in cybersecurity is promising yet filled with challenges. As AI technologies advance, so do the tactics of cybercriminals, who also begin to utilize AI for malicious purposes. This arms race between cyber defenders and attackers underlines the need for continuous innovation and ethical consideration in the field of AI-driven cybersecurity.

Conclusion

The integration of Artificial Intelligence into cybersecurity represents a major leap forward in the fight against cyber threats. AI's role in threat detection and response is not just an enhancement of existing practices; it's a fundamental shift in how cybersecurity challenges are approached. This chapter provides a comprehensive overview of AI's application in cybersecurity, emphasizing its potential, challenges, and ethical implications. As AI continues to evolve, it will undoubtedly shape the future of cybersecurity, making its understanding essential for anyone in the field.

CHAPTER 10:
CRYPTOGRAPHY AND SECURE COMMUNICATION

Introduction

Cryptography, the practice of secure communication in the presence of third parties, is a fundamental element of modern cybersecurity. It involves techniques and protocols to encrypt and decrypt information, ensuring that data remains confidential and integral during transmission. This chapter explores the essential aspects of cryptography and its role in secure communication.

The Basics of Cryptography

Cryptography is divided into several types, each with its unique use case:

- **Symmetric-key cryptography:** Uses the same key for encryption and decryption, suitable for closed systems where secure key sharing is feasible.

- **Asymmetric-key cryptography:** Involves a pair of keys, a public key for encryption and a private key for decryption, facilitating secure communication over unsecured channels.

- **Hash functions:** Provide a one-way transformation to a fixed-size string, which represents the original data uniquely but doesn't allow for its retrieval.

Encryption Techniques

1. **Data Encryption Standard (DES) and Advanced Encryption Standard (AES):**

   - DES, once a widely used symmetric-key algorithm, has largely been superseded by AES due to its higher security level.

   - AES is the current global standard for encrypting sensitive data, offering robust security with various key sizes.

2. **Rivest-Shamir-Adleman (RSA) Algorithm:**

   - A widely used asymmetric encryption algorithm, RSA is key in secure data transmission and digital signatures.

3. **Public Key Infrastructure (PKI):**

   - PKI provides a framework for digital certificates and public key encryption, establishing a trusted method of identity verification in digital communications.

Secure Communication Protocols

- **Secure Sockets Layer (SSL) and Transport Layer Security (TLS):**

   - These protocols provide secure communication over a computer network. They are commonly used for internet browsing, email, and voice-over-IP (VoIP) services.

- **Pretty Good Privacy (PGP) and GNU Privacy Guard (GPG):**

    - PGP and its open-source equivalent GPG offer encryption for securing emails and files, using a combination of symmetric and asymmetric cryptography.

- **Internet Protocol Security (IPSec):**

    - IPSec is used to secure Internet Protocol (IP) communications, encrypting and authenticating all IP packet transfers.

Challenges in Cryptography

Despite its strengths, cryptography faces several challenges:

- **Quantum Computing:** Future quantum computers could potentially break current cryptographic algorithms.

- **Key Management:** Securely managing and storing cryptographic keys remains a significant challenge.

- **Regulatory Compliance:** Navigating the complex landscape of laws and regulations governing encryption across different jurisdictions.

Emerging Trends

The field of cryptography is continually evolving, with current trends including:

- **Homomorphic Encryption:** Allows computation on encrypted data without needing to decrypt it.

- **Quantum Cryptography:** Uses principles of quantum mechanics to develop theoretically unbreakable encryption methods.

Conclusion

Cryptography is the linchpin of secure communication in the digital world. It protects data confidentiality, integrity, and authenticity, forming the foundation of trust in digital interactions. This chapter provides an in-depth look into the various aspects of cryptography and its critical role in cybersecurity. Understanding and implementing effective cryptographic techniques and protocols are essential for protecting information in an increasingly interconnected world.

CHAPTER 11:
NETWORK SECURITY FUNDAMENTALS

Introduction

In an era where networks form the backbone of countless operations, securing them is paramount. Network security is a broad field encompassing various strategies and practices to prevent and monitor unauthorized access, misuse, or modification of a computer network and network-accessible resources. This chapter provides a comprehensive overview of network security fundamentals, focusing on both wired and wireless networks.

Understanding Network Security

Network security involves a set of rules and configurations designed to protect the integrity, confidentiality, and accessibility of computer networks and data using both software and hardware technologies. The goal is to create a secure infrastructure for devices, applications, and users.

Securing Wired Networks

Wired networks, while more controlled than wireless, still face significant security challenges. Essential security measures include:

- **Firewalls:** Act as a barrier between the trusted internal network and untrusted external networks, controlling incoming and outgoing network traffic based on an applied rule set.

- **Intrusion Detection Systems (IDS):** Monitor network traffic for suspicious activity and issue alerts when such activity is detected.

- **Network Segmentation:** Divides the network into smaller parts, making it easier to manage and secure.

- **Virtual Private Networks (VPNs):** Create a secure connection over the internet, encrypting data as it travels between the user and the network.

- **Regular Updates and Patch Management:** Ensures that all systems and applications are up-to-date, reducing the risk of vulnerabilities.

Securing Wireless Networks

Wireless networks pose additional challenges due to their nature. Key strategies for securing wireless networks include:

- **Wireless Network Encryption:** Using protocols like WPA3 (Wi-Fi Protected Access 3) to encrypt data transmitted over wireless networks.

- **Secure Wi-Fi Access Points:** Implementing strong passwords, changing default settings, and disabling WPS (Wi-Fi Protected Setup) to reduce vulnerabilities.

- **Use of Network Access Control (NAC):** To restrict access to the network based on the user's profile and credentials.

- **Monitoring and Testing:** Regularly scanning for unauthorized access points (rogue APs) and conducting penetration testing to evaluate the security of the wireless network.

Best Practices for Network Security

To maintain robust network security, it's crucial to follow best practices, such as:

- **Implementing Strong Authentication Protocols:** Using multi-factor authentication to enhance security.

- **Conducting Regular Security Audits:** To identify and rectify potential vulnerabilities.

- **Employee Training and Awareness:** Ensuring that all users are aware of the potential risks and best practices for network security.

- **Developing and Implementing a Comprehensive Security Policy:** That covers all aspects of the network's security.

Emerging Trends and Future Considerations

The field of network security is rapidly evolving with new technologies. The rise of the Internet of Things (IoT), increased use of cloud services, and advancements in AI and machine learning are shaping the future of network security, introducing new complexities and challenges.

Conclusion

Network security is a critical aspect of modern cybersecurity. Securing both wired and wireless networks requires a comprehensive approach that encompasses a range of strategies, tools, and best practices. This chapter provides a foundational understanding of network security, equipping readers with the knowledge to protect networks against the myriad of threats in today's digital landscape. As technology continues to evolve, staying abreast of the latest trends and developments in network security will be essential for safeguarding digital assets.

CHAPTER 12:
CLOUD SECURITY

Introduction

The advent of cloud computing has revolutionized the way businesses and individuals store and process data, offering scalability, efficiency, and cost-effectiveness. However, this shift to cloud environments has also introduced unique security challenges. This chapter focuses on cloud security, outlining the challenges and strategies necessary for protecting data in cloud environments.

Understanding Cloud Security

Cloud security refers to the set of policies, controls, procedures, and technologies that work together to protect cloud-based systems, data, and infrastructure. It encompasses various aspects of security such as data privacy, compliance, infrastructure security, and identity and access management.

Challenges in Cloud Environments

1. **Data Breaches and Data Loss:** One of the most significant threats in cloud computing, where sensitive data can be exposed or lost.

2. **Insufficient Identity, Credential, and Access Management:** Unauthorized access to cloud services can lead to significant security risks.

3. **Insecure Interfaces and APIs:** Weaknesses in interfaces and APIs can be exploited by attackers.

4. **System Vulnerabilities:** Cloud services can be compromised through system vulnerabilities, leading to data breaches or service disruptions.

5. **Account Hijacking:** Attackers may gain access to users' cloud accounts and manipulate data, eavesdrop on transactions, or direct clients to illegitimate sites.

Strategies for Cloud Security

1. **Data Encryption:** Encrypting data in transit and at rest to protect sensitive information.

2. **Access Control:** Implementing robust authentication and authorization practices to control access to cloud resources.

3. **Firewalls and Intrusion Detection/Prevention Systems:** Deploying firewalls and IDS/IPS tailored for cloud environments.

4. **Regular Security Assessments:** Conducting periodic security assessments to identify and mitigate potential vulnerabilities.

5. **Employee Training and Awareness:** Educating employees about cloud security best practices and potential threats.

Cloud Service Models and Security

- **Infrastructure as a Service (IaaS):** Clients are responsible for securing the operating systems, applications, and data.

- **Platform as a Service (PaaS):** Clients manage the applications and data while the service provider secures the underlying infrastructure.

- **Software as a Service (SaaS):** The service provider is responsible for most aspects of security, but clients must still secure their user accounts and data.

Compliance and Legal Considerations in Cloud Security

Compliance with industry standards and legal requirements is a critical aspect of cloud security. Regulations such as GDPR, HIPAA, and others mandate specific security and privacy measures.

Emerging Trends in Cloud Security

Advancements in AI and machine learning are being leveraged for predictive threat modeling and anomaly detection in cloud environments. The growing adoption of multi-cloud and hybrid cloud strategies also introduces new complexities in cloud security.

Conclusion

Cloud security is an evolving field that requires a strategic approach, encompassing technological, procedural, and educational aspects. As the reliance on cloud computing grows, so does the importance of robust cloud security measures. This chapter provides a comprehensive guide to understanding the challenges and strategies of cloud security, serving as a crucial resource for navigating this complex landscape. With the right approaches and vigilance, it is possible to reap the benefits of cloud computing while mitigating its risks.

CHAPTER 13:
CYBERSECURITY POLICIES AND GOVERNANCE

Introduction

In the complex and ever-evolving landscape of cybersecurity, establishing robust policies and governance structures is critical. Cybersecurity policies are formalized rules within an organization to protect information technology and data assets. This chapter delves into the intricacies of developing and implementing effective cybersecurity policies and governance structures to ensure comprehensive protection and compliance.

The Importance of Cybersecurity Policies

Cybersecurity policies are the backbone of an organization's security posture. They provide clear guidelines on the management of IT resources, define the roles and responsibilities of employees, and establish protocols for responding to cybersecurity incidents. Effective policies are essential not only for security but also for legal compliance and operational efficiency.

Key Elements of Cybersecurity Policies

1. **Scope and Purpose:** Clearly define what the policy covers and its objectives.

2. **Data Classification and Handling:** Outline procedures for handling data based on its sensitivity and criticality.

3. **Access Control:** Set rules for who can access what information and under what conditions.

4. **Incident Response:** Establish procedures for responding to cybersecurity incidents, including roles and responsibilities.

5. **User Education and Awareness:** Include provisions for ongoing staff training on cybersecurity best practices.

Developing Cybersecurity Policies

The development of cybersecurity policies involves several key steps:

- **Risk Assessment:** Identify potential risks to the organization's information assets.

- **Stakeholder Involvement:** Engage various stakeholders across the organization for their input and buy-in.

- **Policy Drafting:** Write the policy, ensuring clarity, comprehensiveness, and alignment with business objectives and compliance requirements.

- **Review and Approval:** Have the policy reviewed by legal, IT, and executive teams before formal approval.

Implementing Cybersecurity Policies

Effective implementation of cybersecurity policies requires:

- **Communication and Training:** Ensure that all employees are aware of the policies and understand their importance.

- **Regular Updates:** Keep the policies up-to-date with evolving cybersecurity threats and business changes.

- **Enforcement:** Implement measures to ensure compliance with the policies, including regular audits and disciplinary actions for violations.

Governance in Cybersecurity

Cybersecurity governance involves the framework and processes that ensure cybersecurity policies are effectively integrated into an organization's operations. It includes:

- **Leadership Commitment:** Strong support from top management is essential for effective governance.

- **Roles and Responsibilities:** Clearly defined roles and responsibilities for cybersecurity within the organization.

- **Performance Metrics:** Establish metrics to measure the effectiveness of cybersecurity efforts.

Legal and Regulatory Compliance

Cybersecurity policies must align with legal and regulatory requirements. Understanding and incorporating relevant laws and standards, such as GDPR, HIPAA, or ISO 27001, is crucial.

Emerging Trends and Future Considerations

The increasing adoption of cloud services, IoT, and AI in businesses brings new challenges and complexities in policy development and governance. Policies must evolve to address these emerging technologies and the unique risks they present.

Conclusion

Developing and implementing effective cybersecurity policies and governance structures are pivotal for any organization's security strategy. These policies serve as a guide for protecting digital assets, ensuring legal compliance, and fostering a security-conscious culture. This chapter offers a comprehensive framework for understanding, drafting, and enforcing cybersecurity policies, emphasizing their critical role in the overall cybersecurity posture of an organization. As the cyber landscape continues to shift, staying agile and informed in policy-making will be key to maintaining robust defenses.

CHAPTER 14:
CYBERSECURITY RISK MANAGEMENT

Introduction

In the dynamic world of cybersecurity, risk management is a fundamental process that helps organizations identify, assess, and mitigate the risks to their information assets. Effective risk management is vital to safeguarding an organization's data, reputation, and operations. This chapter explores the strategies and methodologies of cybersecurity risk management, focusing on the identification and mitigation of risks.

Understanding Cybersecurity Risks

Cybersecurity risks are potential threats that could exploit vulnerabilities in an organization's systems and networks, leading to damage or loss. These risks can originate from various sources, including external threats like hackers and internal threats like employee error.

The Process of Risk Management

Cybersecurity risk management involves several key steps:

1. **Risk Identification:** This initial phase involves recognizing potential cybersecurity threats and vulnerabilities. Methods include system audits, vulnerability assessments, and monitoring threat intelligence.

2. **Risk Analysis and Evaluation:** Assess the potential impact and likelihood of identified risks. This analysis considers factors like the sensitivity of data, system criticality, and existing security controls.

3. **Risk Treatment:** Developing strategies to mitigate identified risks. This could include applying security controls, transferring risk (e.g., through insurance), avoiding risk, or accepting it when the cost of mitigation exceeds the potential impact.

4. **Implementation of Controls:** Implementing appropriate security measures to manage the risks. These controls can be preventive, detective, or corrective.

5. **Monitoring and Review:** Regularly monitoring the effectiveness of risk management strategies and revising them as necessary in response to new threats or changes in the organization.

Risk Mitigation Strategies

Effective risk mitigation in cybersecurity involves a combination of technical, administrative, and physical controls, such as:

- **Technical Controls:** Firewalls, antivirus software, encryption, intrusion detection systems.

- **Administrative Controls:** Policies, procedures, employee training, and awareness programs.

- **Physical Controls:** Secure access to facilities and hardware security.

Importance of a Risk Management Framework

A risk management framework provides a structured approach to managing cybersecurity risks. Popular frameworks include the NIST Cybersecurity Framework, ISO 27001/27002, and the CIS Controls. These frameworks offer best practices and guidelines to manage cybersecurity risks effectively.

Integrating Risk Management with Business Objectives

Effective cybersecurity risk management should align with the organization's overall business objectives and strategy. This alignment ensures that security measures support business goals without imposing unnecessary restrictions or costs.

Emerging Challenges in Risk Management

As technology evolves, new challenges arise in risk management. The proliferation of IoT devices, cloud computing, and AI technologies introduces complex risk scenarios that must be anticipated and managed.

Conclusion

Cybersecurity risk management is a continuous, evolving process that is essential for protecting an organization's information assets. It involves identifying potential risks, assessing their impact, implementing appropriate controls, and continuously monitoring and adjusting these controls. This chapter provides a comprehensive guide to understanding and implementing effective risk management practices in cybersecurity. As the digital landscape changes, so must the strategies to manage the associated risks, making adaptable and proactive risk management an indispensable aspect of modern cybersecurity.

CHAPTER 15:
INCIDENT RESPONSE AND DISASTER RECOVERY

Introduction

The ability to respond effectively to cybersecurity incidents and recover from disasters is crucial for maintaining the resilience of any organization. Incident response and disaster recovery are essential components of a comprehensive cybersecurity strategy. This chapter examines the critical aspects of planning and executing response strategies to mitigate the impact of cyber incidents and ensure swift recovery.

Understanding Incident Response

Incident response is the methodology used to handle and manage the aftermath of a security breach or cyberattack. The aim is to limit damage and reduce recovery time and costs.

Key Stages of Incident Response

1. **Preparation:** Developing an incident response plan, training the response team, and establishing communication protocols.

2. **Identification:** Detecting and determining the nature and scope of the incident.

3. **Containment:** Implementing measures to limit the extent of the incident.

4. **Eradication:** Finding and eliminating the root cause of the incident.

5. **Recovery:** Restoring and returning affected systems and services to their fully operational status.

6. **Lessons Learned:** Reviewing and analyzing the incident to improve future response efforts.

Building an Effective Incident Response Team

An effective incident response team is a cross-functional group that includes IT professionals, security experts, legal counsel, and communication personnel. The team is responsible for executing the incident response plan and should be trained and equipped to handle various cybersecurity incidents.

Disaster Recovery Planning

Disaster recovery involves policies and procedures that enable the recovery or continuation of vital technology infrastructure and systems following a natural or human-induced disaster. A disaster recovery plan (DRP) outlines how an organization will recover from a significant disruptive event.

Components of a Disaster Recovery Plan

- **Risk Assessment and Business Impact Analysis (BIA):** Identifying the impacts of disruptive events and prioritizing recovery efforts.

- **Recovery Strategies:** Developing strategies for IT infrastructure, applications, data, and communication.

- **Plan Development:** Documenting the disaster recovery procedures and protocols.

- **Testing and Maintenance:** Regularly testing the DRP to ensure its effectiveness and updating it as necessary.

Integrating Incident Response with Disaster Recovery

While incident response and disaster recovery are distinct processes, they should be integrated for seamless management of any major incident. This integration ensures that the transition from incident response (handling the immediate effects of an incident) to disaster recovery (long-term recovery and restoration) is smooth and efficient.

The Role of Technology in Response and Recovery

Advancements in technology, such as cloud computing and automated backup solutions, play a vital role in enhancing the effectiveness of response and recovery strategies. They provide more agile, scalable, and reliable platforms for ensuring business continuity.

Challenges in Incident Response and Disaster Recovery

Challenges include rapidly evolving cyber threats, the complexity of IT environments, and the need for compliance with various regulations. Continuous training, testing, and updating of plans are essential to address these challenges effectively.

Conclusion

Incident response and disaster recovery are critical for maintaining the operational integrity and resilience of organizations in the face of cyber threats. This chapter provides a comprehensive overview of planning, executing, and maintaining effective response and recovery strategies. As cybersecurity threats continue to evolve, the importance of robust incident response and disaster recovery plans cannot be overstated. These plans are vital in minimizing the impact of incidents, ensuring rapid recovery, and maintaining trust and confidence among stakeholders.

CHAPTER 16:
EMERGING TECHNOLOGIES AND CYBERSECURITY

Introduction

The ever-evolving landscape of technology brings forth new advancements that hold the potential to revolutionize industries. However, these emerging technologies also introduce new challenges and complexities in cybersecurity. This chapter delves into how the Internet of Things (IoT), blockchain, and quantum computing are reshaping the cybersecurity landscape, highlighting the opportunities and challenges they present.

Internet of Things (IoT) and Cybersecurity

The Internet of Things (IoT) refers to the network of physical devices, vehicles, home appliances, and other items embedded with electronics, software, sensors, actuators, and connectivity. While IoT offers immense opportunities for innovation and efficiency, it also presents significant security challenges.

Challenges:

- **Device Security:** Many IoT devices lack basic security features, making them vulnerable to attacks.

- **Data Privacy:** The vast amount of data generated by IoT devices raises concerns about privacy and data protection.

- **Network Security:** The increased connectivity expands the attack surface for cyber threats.

Strategies:

- **Robust Security Standards:** Developing and adhering to strict security standards for IoT devices.

- **Regular Updates and Patch Management:** Ensuring firmware and software are regularly updated.

- **Secure Network Architectures:** Implementing secure network designs that can isolate and protect IoT devices.

Blockchain Technology and Cybersecurity

Blockchain is a decentralized digital ledger technology known for its security features, primarily used in cryptocurrency systems like Bitcoin. Its implications for cybersecurity are profound.

Opportunities:

- **Data Integrity:** Blockchain ensures data integrity due to its immutable nature.

- **Decentralization:** Reduces the risk of centralized points of failure that hackers can exploit.

- **Smart Contracts:** Can automate security processes with pre-defined conditions.

Challenges:

- **Scalability:** Blockchain networks face challenges in scaling while maintaining security.

- **Regulatory Compliance:** Navigating the regulatory landscape can be complex due to the decentralized nature of blockchain.

Quantum Computing and Cybersecurity

Quantum computing utilizes the principles of quantum theory, holding the potential to process complex data at unprecedented speeds. This poses both opportunities and challenges for cybersecurity.

Challenges:

- **Encryption Threat:** Quantum computing could potentially break current cryptographic algorithms, rendering traditional encryption methods obsolete.

- **New Attack Vectors:** Quantum computers may enable new types of cyberattacks that are currently unfeasible.

Opportunities:

- **Quantum Cryptography:** Quantum key distribution (QKD) offers a new paradigm for secure communication.

- **Enhanced Security Algorithms:** Quantum computing can develop more complex algorithms that are resistant to quantum attacks.

Conclusion

Emerging technologies like IoT, blockchain, and quantum computing are transforming the cybersecurity landscape. They bring innovative solutions to existing problems but also introduce new challenges that require proactive and evolving cybersecurity strategies. Understanding the interplay between these technologies and cybersecurity is crucial for organizations to harness their potential while safeguarding against emerging cyber threats. This chapter provides a comprehensive overview of these technologies and their implications for cybersecurity, offering insights into navigating the challenges and opportunities they present in the digital age.

CHAPTER 17:
CYBERSECURITY CAREER PATHS

Introduction

As the digital world expands and cyber threats evolve, the demand for skilled cybersecurity professionals has surged. The field of cybersecurity offers a wide range of career paths, each playing a crucial role in protecting information systems and data. This chapter explores the diverse roles and responsibilities in the cybersecurity realm, offering insights for those aspiring to enter this dynamic and vital field.

Cybersecurity Analyst

Role: Cybersecurity analysts are the sentinels of the digital world. They monitor networks and systems for security breaches, investigate any potential security incidents, and implement protective measures.

Responsibilities:

- Monitoring security access.

- Conducting security assessments through vulnerability testing and risk analysis.

- Reporting security breaches and assessing their damage.

- Implementing and maintaining security measures and controls.

Penetration Tester

Role: Penetration testers, or ethical hackers, simulate cyber attacks to identify and fix vulnerabilities in security systems before malicious hackers can exploit them.

Responsibilities:

- Conducting simulated attacks to identify vulnerabilities.

- Reporting on findings and recommending improvements.

- Staying updated on the latest methods attackers are using to infiltrate computer systems.

Security Architect

Role: A security architect is responsible for designing, building, and overseeing the implementation of network and computer security for an organization.

Responsibilities:

- Planning, researching, and designing robust security architectures.

- Developing and implementing security policies and procedures.

- Supervising the installation of security systems.

Chief Information Security Officer (CISO)

Role: The CISO is a senior-level executive responsible for establishing and maintaining an organization's vision, strategy, and program to ensure information assets are adequately protected.

Responsibilities:

- Developing and implementing an organization's information security strategy.

- Liaising between the IT department and upper management.

- Managing the IT security team and overseeing all IT security-related activities.

Incident Responder

Role: Incident responders are the first line of defense when a security breach occurs. They manage the aftermath of a security breach or attack.

Responsibilities:

- Responding to cybersecurity incidents and mitigating damage.

- Conducting post-incident analysis to prevent future attacks.

- Keeping detailed logs of incidents and responses.

Forensic Computer Analyst

Role: Forensic computer analysts gather and analyze evidence from computers and other digital devices to solve cybercrimes and aid in legal proceedings.

Responsibilities:

- Recovering data from damaged or deleted files.

- Analyzing data to uncover the extent of a breach or identify the perpetrator.

- Preparing evidence for legal cases.

Cybersecurity Consultant

Role: Consultants offer expert advice to organizations on how to protect their IT infrastructure from cyber threats.

Responsibilities:

- Assessing cybersecurity risks, problems, and solutions for different organizations.

- Providing training and guidance on cybersecurity matters.

- Offering recommendations for security enhancements.

Emerging Roles in Cybersecurity

As technology evolves, new cybersecurity roles emerge, including:

- **IoT Security Specialist:** Focuses on securing interconnected devices.

- **AI Security Specialist:** Develops AI-driven security tools and strategies.

Conclusion

Cybersecurity offers a variety of rewarding career paths for individuals passionate about technology and security. From frontline defenders to strategic planners, each role requires a unique set of skills and plays a critical part in protecting digital assets. This chapter provides an overview of the diverse career opportunities in cybersecurity, highlighting the roles, responsibilities, and significance of these positions in the contemporary digital landscape. Whether starting a career or looking to specialize, the field of cybersecurity offers a dynamic and impactful professional journey.

CHAPTER 18:
EDUCATION AND CERTIFICATION IN CYBERSECURITY

Introduction

In the rapidly evolving field of cybersecurity, education, and certification play a crucial role in shaping competent professionals equipped to tackle diverse security challenges. This chapter explores the various educational pathways and certifications available in cybersecurity, guiding individuals interested in entering or advancing in this dynamic field.

Cybersecurity Degree Programs

1. **Undergraduate Degrees:** Bachelor's programs in cybersecurity, computer science, or related fields provide foundational knowledge in IT, network security, and information assurance.

2. **Graduate Degrees:** Master's programs offer advanced studies in cybersecurity, focusing on areas like cyber operations, information assurance, or digital forensics.

3. **Doctorate Degrees:** PhD programs are research-focused and suitable for those aiming for academic, research, or high-level industry positions.

The Role of Academic Education in Cybersecurity

Academic education provides comprehensive knowledge and theoretical background, making it suitable for understanding complex cybersecurity concepts and developing strategic thinking skills. Degree programs often cover:

- Fundamentals of computing and information technology.

- Network and systems security principles.

- Legal and ethical issues in cybersecurity.

- Advanced topics like cryptography and secure software development.

Cybersecurity Certifications

Certifications are crucial for professionals seeking to demonstrate their skills and expertise in specific areas of cybersecurity. Popular certifications include:

1. **CompTIA Security+:** An entry-level certification covering basic security concepts and best practices.

2. **Certified Information Systems Security Professional (CISSP):** A widely recognized advanced certification for experienced professionals focusing on security management and operations.

3. **Certified Ethical Hacker (CEH):** Focuses on penetration testing and ethical hacking techniques.

4. **Certified Information Security Manager (CISM):** Ideal for IT professionals aspiring to move into management roles, emphasizing security risk management.

5. **Cisco Certified CyberOps Associate:** Focuses on operational aspects of cybersecurity, including monitoring and responding to security incidents.

Specialized Certifications

For those interested in specialized areas, certifications include:

- **Certified Cloud Security Professional (CCSP):** For expertise in cloud security.

- **Offensive Security Certified Professional (OSCP):** For advanced penetration testing skills.

The Importance of Continuous Learning

Cybersecurity is a field that is continuously evolving with new technologies and threats. Therefore, continuous learning through workshops, webinars, and conferences is essential to stay updated with the latest trends and practices.

Choosing the Right Path

The choice between academic education and certification depends on individual career goals:

- Those new to the field may benefit from degree programs for foundational knowledge.

- Professionals looking to specialize or advance in their careers might find certifications more beneficial.

Conclusion

Education and certification in cybersecurity are pivotal for developing the necessary knowledge and skills to face modern cybersecurity challenges. This chapter provides a comprehensive guide on the various educational pathways and certifications available, highlighting their significance and role in forging successful careers in cybersecurity. Whether just starting out or seeking to deepen expertise, the right combination of education and certification can pave the way to a rewarding career in cybersecurity.

CHAPTER 19:
THE FUTURE OF CYBERSECURITY JOBS

Introduction

As technology continues to advance and integrate into every facet of life, the field of cybersecurity is experiencing unprecedented growth and transformation. The future of cybersecurity jobs is shaped by emerging technologies, evolving cyber threats, and the growing complexity of the digital landscape. This chapter explores the trends and predictions that are shaping the future of cybersecurity jobs, offering insights for those looking to navigate and excel in this dynamic field.

Rising Demand for Cybersecurity Professionals

The global increase in cyber threats has led to a surge in demand for skilled cybersecurity professionals. This demand is expected to grow, with predictions indicating a significant shortfall in qualified cybersecurity personnel in the coming years.

Emerging Roles and Specializations

As cybersecurity evolves, new roles and specializations are emerging, including:

- **AI and Machine Learning Security Specialists:** Focusing on integrating AI into cybersecurity strategies.

- **IoT Security Experts:** Specializing in securing interconnected devices and networks.

- **Cloud Security Architects:** Experts in cloud infrastructure protection and cloud-based security solutions.

- **Quantum Computing Security Analysts:** Preparing for the cybersecurity implications of quantum computing.

The Impact of Automation

Automation and AI are transforming many aspects of cybersecurity, leading to a shift in job roles. While automation may streamline routine tasks, the need for professionals with skills in managing and interpreting automated systems will increase.

The Importance of Soft Skills

Alongside technical expertise, soft skills such as problem-solving, analytical thinking, and communication are becoming increasingly important. Cybersecurity professionals must be able to convey complex security concepts to non-technical stakeholders and participate in cross-functional teams.

Continuous Learning and Adaptability

Given the rapid pace of technological change, continuous learning is essential. Cybersecurity professionals must stay abreast of the latest trends, threats, and technologies, adapting their skills accordingly.

Remote Work and Global Opportunities

The shift towards remote work is opening global opportunities for cybersecurity professionals. Companies are increasingly willing to hire remote cybersecurity talent, expanding job prospects beyond geographical boundaries.

Cybersecurity as a Business Enabler

There is a growing recognition of cybersecurity not just as a protective measure but as a strategic business enabler. This shift is creating roles focused on aligning cybersecurity strategies with business objectives.

Increasing Emphasis on Privacy

With rising concerns over data privacy and the proliferation of privacy regulations like GDPR, there is an increased demand for professionals specializing in privacy and compliance.

Conclusion

The future of cybersecurity jobs is marked by exciting opportunities and challenges. The field is not only growing but also diversifying, with new roles and specializations emerging in response to the evolving digital landscape. For those aspiring to a career in cybersecurity, staying informed about these trends, continuously developing both technical and soft skills, and being adaptable to change are key to success. This chapter offers a comprehensive look at the future of cybersecurity jobs, guiding professionals and aspirants in shaping their career paths in this ever-evolving field.

CHAPTER 20:
BUILDING A CYBERSECURITY TEAM

Introduction

In the face of escalating cyber threats, building a robust cybersecurity team is more critical than ever. This chapter delves into the intricacies of assembling a team equipped to defend against and respond to cybersecurity challenges, covering recruitment, training, and management strategies.

Recruitment: Finding the Right Talent

Recruiting the right talent is the first step in building an effective cybersecurity team. The process involves:

1. **Identifying Skill Gaps:** Understanding the specific cybersecurity skills and expertise needed within the organization.

2. **Diverse Talent Pool:** Looking beyond traditional IT backgrounds to include individuals with diverse experiences and skill sets, such as problem-solving and analytical thinking.

3. **Utilizing Various Hiring Channels:** Leveraging job boards, professional networks, cybersecurity conferences, and educational institutions.

4. **Evaluating Technical and Soft Skills:** Assessing candidates not only for their technical proficiency but also for their communication, teamwork, and adaptability skills.

Training: Enhancing Skills and Knowledge

Continuous training is essential in a field as dynamic as cybersecurity. Key aspects include:

1. **Onboarding Training:** Introducing new team members to the organization's cybersecurity policies, tools, and practices.

2. **Ongoing Education:** Providing opportunities for professional development through workshops, courses, certifications, and conferences.

3. **Simulated Cybersecurity Exercises:** Conducting regular drills and simulations to keep the team sharp and prepared for real-world scenarios.

Management: Leading a Cybersecurity Team

Effective management is crucial to the success of a cybersecurity team. This involves:

1. **Clear Communication:** Establishing open lines of communication for reporting threats, sharing information, and discussing strategies.

2. **Defining Roles and Responsibilities:** Clearly outlining each team member's role to ensure comprehensive coverage of all cybersecurity aspects.

3. **Promoting a Collaborative Environment:** Encouraging teamwork and collaboration to leverage the diverse skills and perspectives within the team.

4. **Supporting Work-Life Balance:** Recognizing the high-stress nature of cybersecurity work and promoting a healthy work-life balance.

Building a Resilient Team Culture

Creating a resilient team culture involves fostering a shared commitment to cybersecurity goals, encouraging innovation and continuous learning, and recognizing and rewarding achievements.

Adapting to Changing Cybersecurity Landscapes

The cybersecurity landscape is constantly evolving, and so must the team. This requires staying informed about the latest threats and trends, adapting strategies, and continuously evaluating and enhancing the team's capabilities.

Measuring Team Performance

Establishing metrics and key performance indicators (KPIs) to measure the effectiveness of the team and individual contributions. Metrics might include response times to incidents, the number of incidents successfully resolved, and employee training levels.

Conclusion

Building a cybersecurity team is a strategic process that requires careful planning, ongoing training, and effective management. It involves assembling a group of skilled professionals, continuously enhancing their capabilities, and fostering a culture of collaboration and resilience. This chapter provides a comprehensive guide to creating a cybersecurity team capable of meeting the complex and ever-changing challenges of the digital world, ensuring the organization's digital assets are protected and secure.

CHAPTER 21:
ETHICAL AND LEGAL CONSIDERATIONS IN CYBERSECURITY

Introduction

Cybersecurity is not just a technical challenge; it's also a field deeply entwined with ethical and legal considerations. As cybersecurity professionals navigate the complex landscape of digital threats, they must also consider the ethical implications and legal requirements of their actions and strategies. This chapter explores the crucial ethical dilemmas and legal frameworks that shape the practice of cybersecurity.

Ethical Considerations in Cybersecurity

The ethical landscape of cybersecurity involves a multitude of considerations:

1. **Privacy vs. Security:** Balancing the need to protect systems and data with respecting user privacy.

2. **Disclosure of Vulnerabilities:** Determining when and how to disclose discovered vulnerabilities responsibly.

3. **Use of Malware and Exploits:** The ethical implications of developing and using tools that could be employed for malicious purposes.

4. **Digital Surveillance:** The ethics of monitoring network activity can raise concerns about user privacy and rights.

Principles for Ethical Cybersecurity Practice

Developing a set of core ethical principles is essential for guiding cybersecurity professionals, including honesty, integrity, respect for privacy, and the pursuit of the public good.

Legal Frameworks in Cybersecurity

Cybersecurity practice is governed by a range of laws and regulations, varying by jurisdiction, which include:

1. **Data Protection Laws:** Regulations like GDPR and CCPA that govern the handling of personal data.

2. **Computer Misuse Acts:** Laws that criminalize unauthorized access to computer systems.

3. **Intellectual Property Laws:** Protecting the rights of software creators while considering fair use and reverse engineering for security purposes.

Legal Compliance and Cybersecurity Operations

Ensuring legal compliance in cybersecurity operations involves:

- Staying informed about relevant laws and regulations.

- Implementing policies and procedures that adhere to these legal requirements.

- Regularly reviewing and updating practices to remain compliant.

The Role of Cybersecurity in Law Enforcement

Cybersecurity professionals may sometimes collaborate with law enforcement in investigating and preventing cybercrimes. This collaboration must respect legal boundaries and user rights.

Handling Sensitive Information

Professionals in cybersecurity often handle sensitive information, which must be managed with the utmost care to maintain confidentiality and integrity.

Emerging Legal Challenges

The legal landscape of cybersecurity is continually evolving, particularly in areas like cross-border data flows, cloud computing, and encryption. Staying abreast of these changes is crucial for legal compliance and ethical practice.

Conclusion

Ethical and legal considerations are fundamental to the practice of cybersecurity. They guide professionals in making decisions that are not only effective in protecting digital assets but also respect the rights and privacy of individuals and comply with legal standards. This chapter underscores the importance of integrating ethical principles and legal compliance into every aspect of cybersecurity, ensuring that professionals are not just technically proficient but also ethically and legally conscientious. As the field of cybersecurity evolves, these considerations will become increasingly complex and significant, requiring ongoing attention and adaptation.

CHAPTER 22:
GLOBAL CYBERSECURITY CHALLENGES

Introduction

In our interconnected world, cybersecurity challenges are not confined by national boundaries. They are global in nature, involving complex issues of cross-border data flow, international laws, and multinational cybersecurity policies. This chapter explores the multifaceted nature of global cybersecurity challenges, focusing on the intricacies of managing cybersecurity in a global context.

Cross-Border Data Flow Challenges

The global nature of the internet means data often crosses international borders. This presents unique challenges:

1. **Jurisdictional Issues:** Determining which country's laws apply to data and cybersecurity incidents.

2. **Data Sovereignty:** Issues arising from storing and processing data in different countries, each with its own legal requirements.

3. **Diverse Regulatory Environments:** Navigating varying data protection regulations, such as GDPR in Europe and varying laws across Asia, Africa, and the Americas.

International Cybersecurity Laws and Cooperation

1. **Extraterritoriality of Laws:** Understanding how laws like the GDPR have extraterritorial implications.

2. **International Cooperation:** The need for countries to collaborate in combating cyber threats, sharing intelligence, and harmonizing legal approaches.

3. **Cyber Diplomacy:** Developing diplomatic solutions to address state-sponsored cyber activities and cyber warfare.

Global Cybersecurity Standards and Best Practices

The development of international cybersecurity standards and best practices is crucial. This includes frameworks like ISO/IEC 27001 for information security management.

Challenges in Enforcing Global Cybersecurity

1. **Differing National Priorities:** Balancing national security interests with global cybersecurity cooperation.

2. **Asymmetric Cyber Capabilities:** Addressing disparities in cybersecurity capabilities between developed and developing nations.

3. **Global Supply Chain Security:** Managing risks associated with the global IT supply chain, including hardware and software sourcing.

Emerging Global Cybersecurity Trends

Rapid advancements in technology are shaping global cybersecurity challenges:

- **5G Networks:** Introducing new security considerations with increased speed and connectivity.

- **Internet of Things (IoT):** The proliferation of IoT devices increases the complexity of global cybersecurity.

Cybersecurity in Multinational Corporations

Multinational corporations face the challenge of implementing cohesive cybersecurity strategies across different legal and cultural landscapes. This includes establishing global security policies and ensuring compliance in all operating regions.

The Role of International Agreements and Frameworks

International agreements and frameworks play a crucial role in addressing global cybersecurity challenges. Examples include the Budapest Convention on Cybercrime and various UN initiatives.

Conclusion

Global cybersecurity challenges require a coordinated, multinational approach that respects the complexities of international laws, respects data sovereignty, and fosters global cooperation.

This chapter offers a deep dive into the issues surrounding cross-border data flow and international cybersecurity efforts, highlighting the need for harmonized global strategies. As the digital landscape becomes increasingly borderless, understanding and addressing these global challenges is imperative for creating a secure and resilient cyber environment worldwide.

CHAPTER 23:
CYBERSECURITY AND SOCIETY

Introduction

The intersection of cybersecurity and society is intricate and profound. Cybersecurity isn't just about technology; it's equally about the people who interact with it. This chapter delves into the societal aspects of cybersecurity, focusing on social engineering and the human factors that play a pivotal role in both the creation and prevention of cyber threats.

Understanding Social Engineering

Social engineering is a method of cyber attack that manipulates individuals into breaking normal security procedures. It's a significant threat because it exploits human psychology rather than technical vulnerabilities.

Types of Social Engineering Attacks

1. **Phishing:** The use of deceitful emails or messages to trick individuals into revealing personal information.

2. **Spear Phishing:** Targeted phishing attacks aimed at specific individuals or organizations.

3. **Pretexting:** Fabricating scenarios to steal personal information.

4. **Baiting:** Offering something enticing to compromise security protocols.

5. **Tailgating:** Unauthorized physical access to restricted areas by following authorized personnel.

Human Factors in Cybersecurity

Human factors refer to the psychological and behavioral aspects of cybersecurity:

1. **The Role of Awareness:** Increasing cybersecurity awareness among individuals, especially social engineering, is crucial for preventing attacks.

2. **Training and Education:** Regular training sessions to educate employees about cybersecurity best practices and emerging threats.

3. **The Psychology of Cybersecurity:** Understanding the psychological elements, like trust and authority, which are often exploited in social engineering attacks.

Building a Security-Conscious Culture

Creating a security-conscious culture within organizations and societies involves:

- Promoting a mindset where security is everyone's responsibility.

- Encouraging vigilance and skepticism, especially regarding information sharing.

- Recognizing and rewarding secure behavior.

Social Engineering Defense Strategies

To combat social engineering, several strategies can be employed:

- Implementing strong verification processes.

- Conducting regular social engineering drills.

- Developing clear and straightforward security protocols.

The Impact of Social Media

Social media platforms are fertile ground for social engineering attacks. Awareness about the type of personal information shared on these platforms is crucial for preventing identity theft and other cybercrimes.

Ethical Considerations in Cybersecurity

Cybersecurity professionals face ethical challenges, especially in balancing security needs with individual privacy rights. Ethical hacking, for instance, involves penetrating systems to identify vulnerabilities, but it must be conducted within legal and ethical boundaries.

Future Trends in Social Engineering and Human Factors

Emerging technologies like deepfakes and AI-driven chatbots are likely to make social engineering attacks more sophisticated. Future cybersecurity strategies will need to evolve accordingly, with a greater emphasis on understanding and mitigating human vulnerabilities.

Conclusion

Cybersecurity and society are deeply interconnected, with social engineering highlighting the critical role of human factors in cybersecurity. This chapter underscores the importance of understanding and addressing the human element in cybersecurity. By fostering a security-conscious culture and equipping individuals with the knowledge to recognize and resist social engineering tactics, society can enhance its defense against an ever-evolving array of cyber threats.

CHAPTER 24:
CASE STUDIES IN CYBERSECURITY

Introduction

Real-world case studies in cybersecurity offer invaluable lessons and insights into the nature of cyber threats, the effectiveness of defense strategies, and the consequences of security breaches. This chapter presents an analysis of notable cybersecurity incidents, exploring their impact, the response strategies employed, and the lessons learned from each case.

Case Study 1: The WannaCry Ransomware Attack (2017)

Overview: WannaCry was a global ransomware attack that affected hundreds of thousands of computers across 150 countries. It exploited a vulnerability in Microsoft Windows and encrypted data, demanding ransom for its release.

Analysis:

- Impact: Massive disruptions in various sectors, including healthcare and transportation.

- Response: Emergency patches released by Microsoft and the accidental discovery of a kill switch halted the spread.

- Lessons Learned: The importance of regular software updates, the risks of using unsupported software, and the need for robust backup strategies.

Case Study 2: The Equifax Data Breach (2017)

Overview: Equifax, one of the largest credit bureaus in the U.S., suffered a massive data breach that exposed the personal information of about 147 million people.

Analysis:

- Impact: Compromise of sensitive personal information, leading to lawsuits and regulatory scrutiny.

- Response: Free credit monitoring offered to affected customers and significant changes in leadership and security practices.

- Lessons Learned: The need for proactive vulnerability management, the importance of timely patching of known vulnerabilities, and the critical role of leadership in cybersecurity.

Case Study 3: SolarWinds Supply Chain Attack (2020)

Overview: A sophisticated cyber espionage campaign that targeted the SolarWinds Orion software, affecting multiple U.S. government agencies and businesses.

Analysis:

- Impact: Compromise of sensitive government data and corporate espionage.

- Response: Removal of compromised components, forensic investigations, and bolstering of network defenses.

- Lessons Learned: The risks associated with supply chain attacks, the need for rigorous third-party security assessments, and the value of a multi-layered defense strategy.

Case Study 4: The Colonial Pipeline Ransomware Attack (2021)

Overview: A ransomware attack on Colonial Pipeline, one of the largest pipeline operators in the U.S., led to a significant disruption in fuel supply on the East Coast.

Analysis:

- Impact: Fuel shortages, rise in fuel prices, and declaration of a state of emergency in several states.

- Response: Temporary shutdown of operations, payment of ransom, and enhanced cybersecurity measures.

- Lessons Learned: The critical importance of cybersecurity in critical infrastructure, the consequences of paying ransoms, and the need for incident response planning.

Emerging Trends from Case Studies

- **Ransomware Evolution:** Increasing sophistication and targeting of ransomware attacks.

- **Supply Chain Vulnerabilities:** Growing need to secure the supply chain against cyber threats.

- **Critical Infrastructure Risks:** Highlighting the vulnerability of essential services to cyber attacks.

- **Regulatory and Legal Implications:** Increased regulatory scrutiny and legal consequences following major breaches.

Conclusion

These case studies in cybersecurity provide critical learning opportunities for cybersecurity professionals and organizations. They highlight the evolving nature of threats, underscore the importance of robust security practices, and demonstrate the far-reaching impact of cyber incidents. By analyzing these real-world incidents, the chapter offers valuable insights into developing more effective cybersecurity strategies and preparing for future threats.

CHAPTER 25:
THE ROLE OF GOVERNMENTS IN CYBERSECURITY

Introduction

In the digital era, cybersecurity transcends individual and corporate concerns, becoming a matter of national and international security. Governments around the world play a pivotal role in shaping the cybersecurity landscape, from legislating and enforcing cyber laws to protecting critical national infrastructure and engaging in cyber warfare. This chapter delves into the multifaceted role of governments in cybersecurity, examining their impact on national security and the global cyber warfare arena.

National Cybersecurity Strategies

Governments develop and implement national cybersecurity strategies to protect critical infrastructure, government networks, and sensitive data. These strategies typically involve:

1. **Creating Cybersecurity Frameworks:** Establishing guidelines and standards for cybersecurity practices.
2. **Protecting Critical Infrastructure:** Securing vital sectors such as energy, transportation, and finance.
3. **Information Sharing:** Facilitating the exchange of cybersecurity information between the public and private sectors.
4. **Public Awareness Campaigns:** Educating citizens about cyber threats and safe online practices.

Legislation and Regulation

Governments enact cybersecurity laws and regulations to protect against cybercrimes, safeguard personal data, and ensure the security of digital transactions. Examples include the GDPR in Europe and the Cybersecurity Information Sharing Act (CISA) in the United States.

Cybersecurity Agencies and Task Forces

Many governments have established dedicated agencies and task forces to handle national cybersecurity issues, such as the United States' Cybersecurity and Infrastructure Security Agency (CISA) and the United Kingdom's National Cyber Security Centre (NCSC).

International Collaboration and Diplomacy

Cross-border cyber threats necessitate international collaboration. Governments engage in cyber diplomacy and participate in international forums like the United Nations to develop global cybersecurity norms and agreements.

Cyber Warfare and National Defense

Cyber warfare has become an integral part of national defense strategies. Governments develop offensive and defensive cyber capabilities to protect national interests and engage in cyber operations when necessary.

Challenges Faced by Governments

1. **Rapidly Evolving Threats:** Keeping pace with the fast-evolving nature of cyber threats.

2. **Balancing Security and Privacy:** Ensuring robust cybersecurity measures while respecting citizens' privacy and rights.

3. **Resource Allocation:** Distributing adequate resources for comprehensive national cybersecurity initiatives.

Emerging Trends in Governmental Cybersecurity

- **Increased Use of AI and Machine Learning:** Leveraging advanced technologies for threat detection and response.

- **Focus on Supply Chain Security:** Addressing vulnerabilities in national and global supply chains.

- **Cybersecurity in the Era of IoT:** Securing the increasing number of connected devices.

Conclusion

The role of governments in cybersecurity is complex and multifaceted, encompassing national security, legal and regulatory frameworks, international collaboration, and cyber warfare. As the cyber landscape continues to evolve, governments must adapt and respond to new challenges, ensuring the security and resilience of national infrastructures and systems. This chapter provides an in-depth exploration of the various roles governments play in the realm of cybersecurity, highlighting their critical impact on both national and global cybersecurity postures.

CHAPTER 26:
PUBLIC AWARENESS AND CYBERSECURITY EDUCATION

Introduction

The human element is often the weakest link in cybersecurity. Enhancing public awareness and education is crucial for building a more secure digital world. This chapter explores the importance of community outreach and awareness programs in fostering a widespread understanding of cybersecurity risks and best practices.

The Necessity of Cybersecurity Education

In an age where digital interactions are integral to daily life, a lack of cybersecurity awareness can lead to significant vulnerabilities. Educating the public about cyber risks and safe online practices is essential for protecting individuals and communities from cyber threats.

Community Outreach Initiatives

1. **Cybersecurity Workshops and Seminars:** Offering free or low-cost workshops to educate the public on basic cybersecurity concepts.

2. **School Programs:** Integrating cybersecurity education in school curricula to build awareness from a young age.

3. **Partnerships with Local Businesses:** Collaborating with local businesses to spread cybersecurity awareness in the community.

Creating Effective Awareness Campaigns

Effective cybersecurity awareness campaigns should:

- Be relatable and understandable to the general public.

- Use a variety of mediums, such as social media, print, and community events, to reach a broader audience.

- Provide practical and actionable advice.

- Highlight the consequences of poor cybersecurity practices.

Role of Governments and Nonprofits in Cybersecurity Education

Governments and nonprofit organizations play a pivotal role in cybersecurity education by:

- Funding cybersecurity awareness initiatives.

- Developing national cybersecurity awareness campaigns.

- Providing resources and support for cybersecurity education in schools and communities.

Online Resources and Digital Literacy

Promoting digital literacy is a significant aspect of cybersecurity education. Online resources, including websites, tutorials, and webinars, can be instrumental in teaching safe online habits and practices.

Challenges in Cybersecurity Education

- **Keeping Content Updated:** Ensuring educational materials reflect the latest cybersecurity trends and threats.

- **Engagement:** Engaging diverse audiences who may not realize the importance of cybersecurity.

- **Resource Allocation:** Obtaining sufficient funding and resources for comprehensive education programs.

Measuring the Impact of Education and Awareness Programs

Assessing the effectiveness of these programs can be challenging but is necessary to improve future initiatives. Metrics may include the number of participants, changes in behavior, and feedback from attendees.

Emerging Trends in Cybersecurity Education

- **Gamification:** Using interactive and game-like elements to make learning about cybersecurity more engaging.

- **Virtual and Augmented Reality:** Providing immersive experiences for cybersecurity training.

- **Customized Learning Pathways:** Offering tailored educational content based on individual knowledge levels and interests.

Conclusion

Public awareness and education are vital in creating a society resilient to cyber threats. This chapter emphasizes the importance of community outreach and awareness programs in building a widespread understanding of cybersecurity. By engaging various stakeholders, including governments, educational institutions, businesses, and the public, these programs play a crucial role in fostering a culture of cybersecurity awareness and preparedness.

CHAPTER 27:
THE BUSINESS OF CYBERSECURITY

Introduction

In the digital age, cybersecurity has transcended its role as a mere protective measure and has emerged as a burgeoning industry ripe with business opportunities. This chapter delves into the dynamic business landscape of cybersecurity, exploring current market trends and the diverse array of business opportunities it presents.

Understanding the Cybersecurity Market

The cybersecurity market is a rapidly expanding sector, influenced by increasing digitalization, evolving cyber threats, and stringent regulatory requirements. It encompasses a range of products and services, from security software and hardware to consulting and managed security services.

Current Market Trends

1. **Rising Demand for Managed Security Services:** Organizations are increasingly outsourcing their security needs to specialized service providers.

2. **Growth in Cloud Security Solutions:** As businesses migrate to the cloud, there is a growing demand for cloud-native security solutions.

3. **Integration of AI and Machine Learning:** Leveraging advanced technologies for predictive threat analysis and intelligent security automation.

4. **Focus on Mobile Security:** With the proliferation of mobile devices, mobile security solutions are becoming essential.

Business Opportunities in Cybersecurity

1. **Security Software Development:** Developing innovative software solutions, such as antivirus programs, firewalls, and encryption tools.

2. **Cybersecurity Consulting:** Providing expert advice to businesses on cybersecurity strategies, risk assessments, and compliance.

3. **Managed Security Services:** Offering outsourced monitoring and management of security devices and systems.

4. **Cybersecurity Training and Education:** Creating training programs for organizations to enhance their internal cybersecurity expertise.

5. **Incident Response Services:** Specializing in emergency response to cyber incidents and data breaches.

Challenges and Considerations for Cybersecurity Businesses

- **Rapidly Changing Threat Landscape:** Staying ahead of evolving cyber threats and adapting solutions accordingly.

- **Competition:** Differentiating in a market with numerous players and rapidly emerging new entrants.

- **Compliance and Regulation:** Navigating a complex and varied regulatory landscape across different regions.

Investment in Cybersecurity Startups

The cybersecurity sector is attracting significant investment, with startups offering innovative solutions and securing funding from venture capitalists and angel investors.

The Role of Cybersecurity in Mergers and Acquisitions

Cybersecurity considerations play a critical role in mergers and acquisitions, with due diligence increasingly including cyber risk assessments.

Future Prospects in the Cybersecurity Market

Emerging technologies like the Internet of Things (IoT) and 5G networks are expected to drive future growth in the cybersecurity market, creating new opportunities for businesses.

Conclusion

The business of cybersecurity is a dynamic and rapidly growing field, presenting a wide array of opportunities for entrepreneurs and established companies alike. This chapter provides a comprehensive overview of the current market trends and business opportunities within the cybersecurity sector. It highlights the importance of innovation, adaptability, and strategic planning in capitalizing on the burgeoning demand for cybersecurity solutions. As digital threats continue to evolve, so too will the opportunities for businesses in this critical and lucrative industry.

CHAPTER 28:
CYBERSECURITY TOOLS AND RESOURCES

Introduction

In the fast-paced and ever-evolving field of cybersecurity, having the right tools and resources is crucial for staying ahead of threats. This chapter provides a comprehensive guide to the various cybersecurity tools, forums, and online resources available for professionals, businesses, and individuals keen on enhancing their cybersecurity posture.

Cybersecurity Software Tools

The backbone of cybersecurity defense lies in a suite of software tools designed for various protective purposes:

1. **Antivirus and Anti-Malware Software:** Essential for detecting and removing malicious software.

2. **Firewalls:** Act as a barrier between secure internal networks and untrusted external networks.

3. **Encryption Tools:** Protect sensitive data by encoding it into an unreadable format.

4. **Intrusion Detection and Prevention Systems (IDPS):** Monitor network traffic for signs of malicious activity.

5. **Vulnerability Scanning Tools:** Identify and report security vulnerabilities in systems and networks.

6. **Security Information and Event Management (SIEM) Systems:** Provide real-time analysis of security alerts generated by applications and network hardware.

Cybersecurity Forums and Communities

Forums and online communities are invaluable for staying updated on the latest threats, trends, and best practices:

1. **Professional Forums:** Platforms like ISACA, (ISC)² and SANS Institute forums where professionals share insights and seek advice.

2. **Reddit Communities:** Subreddits like r/cybersecurity and r/netsec offer vibrant spaces for discussion and news.

3. **LinkedIn Groups:** Professional groups on LinkedIn provide networking opportunities and knowledge sharing.

Online Learning Resources

Continuous learning is vital in cybersecurity. Various online platforms offer courses, tutorials, and certifications:

1. **Cybrary:** A free and community-driven platform offering cybersecurity and IT training.

2. **Coursera and Udemy:** Host a variety of courses ranging from introductory to advanced levels.

3. **MIT OpenCourseWare:** Offers free course materials from MIT's cybersecurity programs.

4. **YouTube Channels:** Channels like Computerphile and Hak5 provide insights and tutorials on cybersecurity topics.

Cybersecurity News and Information Portals

Staying informed about the latest developments in cybersecurity is crucial:

1. **Security Blogs:** Blogs like Krebs on Security, Schneier on Security, and Dark Reading offer in-depth analysis and news.

2. **Industry Reports:** Annual reports from organizations like Verizon (DBIR) and Symantec provide valuable insights into cybersecurity trends.

3. **Government Resources:** Websites like CISA (Cybersecurity and Infrastructure Security Agency) provide alerts and guidance on cybersecurity.

Cybersecurity Podcasts

Podcasts offer a convenient way to stay informed and gain insights from industry experts:

1. **Darknet Diaries:** Explores true stories from the dark side of the Internet.

2. **The CyberWire:** A daily podcast covering cybersecurity news and events.

Collaborative Platforms and Tools

Platforms like GitHub and Stack Overflow allow cybersecurity professionals to collaborate on projects, share code, and solve problems collectively.

Conclusion

The plethora of cybersecurity tools, forums, and online resources available today provides professionals and enthusiasts with the means to enhance their knowledge, stay informed, and effectively protect against cyber threats. This chapter serves as a guide to navigating these resources, emphasizing the importance of ongoing learning and community engagement in the field of cybersecurity. Whether for personal growth, professional development, or organizational security, leveraging these tools and resources is key to building a strong defense in the digital age.

CHAPTER 29:
PREPARING FOR THE FUTURE IN CYBERSECURITY

Introduction

In the realm of cybersecurity, the only constant is change. The rapid evolution of technology, along with the ever-increasing sophistication of cyber threats, demands continuous adaptation and forward-thinking. This chapter addresses strategies and approaches for staying ahead in the dynamic field of cybersecurity, ensuring preparedness for future challenges.

Understanding Emerging Technologies

Staying informed about emerging technologies is critical, as these often shape future cybersecurity landscapes. Key areas include:

1. **Artificial Intelligence and Machine Learning:** Understanding their role in both enhancing cybersecurity measures and the potential for AI-driven threats.

2. **Quantum Computing:** Preparing for its impact on encryption and data security.

3. **Internet of Things (IoT):** Addressing the security challenges posed by the proliferation of connected devices.

4. **Blockchain:** Exploring its applications in securing transactions and data integrity.

Developing a Proactive Security Mindset

A proactive approach involves anticipating future threats and trends rather than reacting to incidents as they occur. This can be achieved through:

1. **Continuous Risk Assessment:** Regularly evaluating and updating security strategies to address emerging threats.

2. **Threat Intelligence Gathering:** Using advanced tools and resources to stay abreast of new cyber threats.

3. **Scenario Planning and War Gaming:** Simulating potential cyber attack scenarios to prepare for real-world incidents.

Fostering a Culture of Cybersecurity

Building a culture of cybersecurity within organizations is vital. It involves:

1. **Regular Training and Awareness Programs:** Educating all levels of staff about the importance of cybersecurity and best practices.

2. **Encouraging Open Communication:** Promoting a culture where employees feel comfortable reporting potential security threats or breaches.

3. **Leadership Involvement:** Ensuring top management recognizes the importance of cybersecurity and allocates appropriate resources.

Investing in Continuous Learning and Development

For cybersecurity professionals, continuous learning is key to staying relevant:

1. **Professional Development:** Pursuing advanced degrees, certifications, and specialized training.

2. **Networking and Community Engagement:** Participating in industry conferences, workshops, and forums.

3. **Research and Publication:** Contributing to cybersecurity research and staying updated with the latest academic and industry insights.

Adopting Agile and Flexible Security Frameworks

Implementing security frameworks that are adaptable to changing technologies and threats is essential. This includes the ability to rapidly update and modify security protocols and systems.

Collaboration and Information Sharing

Collaborating with other organizations, industry groups, and government agencies can enhance collective cybersecurity knowledge and defense capabilities.

Ethical and Legal Considerations

Staying informed about ethical and legal considerations, including data privacy laws and regulations, is crucial in a global and interconnected digital environment.

Conclusion

Preparing for the future in cybersecurity requires a multifaceted approach that encompasses staying informed about technological advancements, fostering a proactive and educated organizational culture, investing in continuous personal and professional development, and embracing collaboration and adaptability. This chapter equips readers with the strategies and mindset necessary to navigate and stay ahead in the rapidly evolving field of cybersecurity. The future of cybersecurity, while challenging, offers tremendous opportunities for those prepared to meet its demands.

CHAPTER 30:
CONCLUSION - THE EVER-EVOLVING LANDSCAPE OF CYBERSECURITY

Summary

The landscape of cybersecurity is a complex and ever-changing realm, continuously shaped and reshaped by technological advancements, evolving cyber threats, and the shifting needs of individuals, organizations, and governments. This book has journeyed through the intricacies of cybersecurity, from its fundamental concepts to the multifaceted roles and responsibilities within its domain. We have explored the challenges and strategies in various sectors, the impact of laws and regulations, the revolutionary role of emerging technologies, and the vital importance of education, awareness, and preparedness.

The Dynamic Nature of Cyber Threats

Cyber threats have evolved from simple viruses to sophisticated state-sponsored attacks, ransomware, and AI-powered phishing schemes. The rapid proliferation of IoT devices and the increasing reliance on cloud services have further expanded the attack surface, necessitating advanced and adaptable cybersecurity strategies.

The Role of AI and Machine Learning

AI and machine learning have emerged as double-edged swords in cybersecurity – tools for both defenders and attackers. These technologies have revolutionized threat detection and response but also opened avenues for more sophisticated attacks.

The Growing Importance of Cybersecurity in Everyday Life

Cybersecurity is no longer just a concern for IT professionals. It has become a critical aspect of everyday life, impacting individuals, businesses, and governments alike. The rise in remote work, e-commerce, and digital communication further underscores the need for robust personal and organizational cybersecurity measures.

The Future Outlook of Cybersecurity

Looking ahead, the field of cybersecurity is poised for continued growth and evolution. Key trends likely to shape the future include:

1. **The Rise of Quantum Computing:** Quantum computing presents potential challenges to current encryption methods, prompting the need for quantum-resistant cryptography.

2. **Increased Focus on Privacy:** As public awareness of data privacy grows, organizations will need to prioritize privacy in their cybersecurity strategies.

3. **Expansion of Cybersecurity Regulations:** Expect more comprehensive and stringent cybersecurity regulations globally, requiring enhanced compliance efforts.

4. **Greater Emphasis on Cyber Resilience:** Organizations will shift from solely focusing on prevention to building resilient systems capable of withstanding and rapidly recovering from attacks.

5. **Human Factor:** The role of human behavior in cybersecurity will gain more focus, emphasizing the need for continuous education and a culture of security awareness.

Conclusion

As we navigate this ever-evolving landscape, the key to success in cybersecurity lies in adaptability, continuous learning, and proactive defense strategies. Collaboration across industries and borders, investment in research and development, and a holistic approach to security are essential in building a safer digital future. This book has aimed to provide a comprehensive understanding of the complex world of cybersecurity, equipping readers with the knowledge and insights needed to navigate and contribute to this critical field. As we look to the future, one thing is certain: cybersecurity will remain an integral and ever-expanding aspect of our digital lives, demanding our constant attention, innovation, and commitment.

CHAPTER 31:
CYBERSECURITY MYTH AND FACTS

Introduction

In the field of cybersecurity, separating myths from facts is crucial for understanding the true nature of cyber threats and the effectiveness of security measures. Misconceptions can lead to complacency, poor decision-making, and inadequate protection strategies. This chapter demystifies common cybersecurity myths, presenting the facts to provide a clearer and more accurate picture of the cybersecurity landscape.

Myth 1: Small Businesses Are Not Targets for Cyber Attacks

Fact: Small businesses are often targets because they may lack the resources for robust security measures, making them easier targets compared to larger organizations. Attackers also exploit smaller businesses as entry points into larger networks.

Myth 2: Antivirus Software Alone Is Sufficient for Protection

Fact: While antivirus software is a vital component of cybersecurity defense, it is not foolproof. Cyber threats often evolve faster than antivirus updates. A multi-layered security approach, including firewalls, behavior-based detection, and regular software updates, is essential.

Myth 3: Cybersecurity Is Solely an IT Issue

Fact: Cybersecurity is a business-wide concern. It requires the involvement of all departments and levels, including executive leadership. Employee awareness and training across the organization are crucial in mitigating cyber risks.

Myth 4: Strong Passwords Are Enough to Keep You Secure

Fact: Strong passwords are important but not infallible. Two-factor authentication (2FA) and other security measures are recommended to add additional layers of security.

Myth 5: Cyber Attacks Are Always Sophisticated

Fact: Many successful cyber-attacks are relatively simple and exploit basic security vulnerabilities, such as unpatched software or human error. Not all attacks involve complex techniques or advanced malware.

Myth 6: Cybersecurity Is Too Expensive for My Business

Fact: The cost of a cyber-attack often far exceeds the cost of preventative measures. Investing in cybersecurity can be cost-effective, especially when considering the potential losses from data breaches.

Myth 7: If You Haven't Been Attacked, You Don't Need to Worry

Fact: Lack of a previous attack does not guarantee future safety. Continuous vigilance and proactive defense are necessary, as the threat landscape is constantly evolving.

Myth 8: A Cyber Attack Is Immediately Obvious

Fact: Many cyber-attacks are designed to be stealthy and may go unnoticed for a long time. Continuous monitoring and regular security assessments are crucial for early detection.

Myth 9: All Cyber Threats Come from External Sources

Fact: Internal threats, whether intentional or accidental, can be as damaging as external attacks. Insider threats need to be considered in a comprehensive cybersecurity strategy.

Myth 10: Compliance with Regulations Equals Complete Security

Fact: While regulatory compliance is important, it should not be the sole focus of cybersecurity efforts. Compliance does not guarantee security; it is a baseline from which to build more comprehensive security practices.

Conclusion

Understanding the facts behind these myths is vital for developing effective cybersecurity strategies. This chapter aims to clarify common misconceptions, providing a more realistic view of the threats and the necessary measures to combat them. By acknowledging and addressing these myths, businesses and individuals can better prepare themselves against the myriad of cyber threats in today's digital world. Cybersecurity is an ever-changing field, and staying informed is key to maintaining robust defenses.

GLOSSARY

1. Antivirus Software: A program designed to detect, prevent, and remove malware and other malicious software.

2. Blockchain: A distributed ledger technology known for its role in cryptocurrency systems and potential applications in secure transactions.

3. Cybersecurity: The practice of protecting systems, networks, and programs from digital attacks.

4. Data Encryption: The process of converting data into a code to prevent unauthorized access.

5. Firewalls: Network security systems that monitor and control incoming and outgoing network traffic based on predetermined security rules.

6. GDPR (General Data Protection Regulation): A regulation in EU law on data protection and privacy in the European Union and the European Economic Area.

7. IoT (Internet of Things): The network of physical objects embedded with sensors, software, and other technologies to connect and exchange data with other devices and systems over the internet.

8. Malware: Malicious software designed to harm, exploit, or damage systems, networks, or data.

9. Phishing: A cybercrime in which targets are contacted by email, telephone, or text message by someone posing as a legitimate institution to lure individuals into providing sensitive data.

10. Ransomware: A type of malicious software designed to block access to a computer system until a sum of money is paid.

11. Two-Factor Authentication (2FA): A security process in which users provide two different authentication factors to verify themselves.

12. VPN (Virtual Private Network): A service that encrypts your internet traffic and protects your online identity.

INDEX

A

- Artificial Intelligence, 82, 150
- Authentication, 45, 98

B

- Blockchain, 75, 130
- Business Continuity, 190

C

- Cloud Security, 120-125
- Cyber Attacks, 30, 85, 180

D

- Data Breach, 29, 90, 188
- Digital Forensics, 60, 145

E

- Encryption, 47, 116
- Ethical Hacking, 65, 140

F

- Firewalls, 48, 113

G

- GDPR, 105, 160